Bags, Hats and Mats!

by Rachel Russ

Plants

Look at the bags, hats and mats!
They all come from plants.

Let's see how they are constructed.

Plants can be transformed into lots of things.

Flax

This plant is flax. Flax is strong and it bends.

Strands of flax can be twisted. It can be turned into the strongest string.

This bag's handles are twisted flax.

Ilala

This ilala plant has fronds.
Fronds have a wax coat.

Fronds can be coiled by hand.

Coils can be formed into a container. They follow a strict pattern.

Pandanus

This is a pandanus tree. It grows near the coast.

Fronds from the top of the tree are harvested.

This will be a bright mat.

Bark

All trees have bark. Bark is the outer part of a tree's trunk.

You can cut bark. Bark sheets can be braided to form bags.

Bamboo

Bamboo stems are strong and hollow. Bamboo can be turned into fabric!

1. Stems are cut into strips.

2. Strips are scrunched into pulp.

3. Pulp is turned into yarn and fabric.

Look at this bamboo chair.

Flax can be transformed into bed sheets.

We construct lots of things from plants.

Can you look for something constructed from a plant?

Look Back

Encourage students to use the images to review the topic.